From Employee to Entrepreneur

Henry Allen

Henry Allen

Copyright Page

Henry Allen

Index

'

Henry Allen

Why do you want to start a business?

Before taking the leap into the world of entrepreneurship, it is essential to ask yourself a simple but powerful question: why do you want to start a business? This question, although it seems basic, has the power to define your success or failure. It is not a question to answer lightly or to throw out empty phrases like "I want to be my own boss" or "I want to earn more money." It is a question that requires brutal honesty with yourself. The answer you give will not only guide your steps, but will be the basis of your motivation on difficult days, because believe me, there will be difficult days.

Maybe you're tired of the routine of a traditional job, the endless traffic, the clock ticking down every second of your day as a reminder of what you could be doing with your life. Maybe you feel like you're trapped in a system that doesn't recognize your potential, in a work environment that doesn't inspire you or, worse yet, that drains you. These reasons are valid, but not enough. If displeasure with your current job is your only motivation to start a business, you're likely to be in for an unpleasant surprise: entrepreneurship is not an easy way out, nor a magic wand that fixes everything you don't like about your life.

Entrepreneurship requires passion, but not just any kind of passion. It's not enough to love the idea of having a business; you must feel deeply connected to the activity you are going to do. Why? Because there will be days when you feel like everything is against you. Days when clients don't come, sales don't happen, or the numbers don't add up. It's in those moments when the real reason you decided to start a business will be your fuel. If you start a business just for money, you might give up at the first obstacle, because money takes time to arrive. If you start a business for recognition, you will find yourself faced with the harsh reality that success is not always visible to others, at least not at first. But if you start a business because you love what you do and because you have a clear vision of what you want to build, it will be easier to stay on course even in the storms.

Another common reason for starting a business is the desire for freedom. And yes, entrepreneurship offers an unparalleled sense of freedom, but it also comes with enormous responsibility. Being your own boss means that everything is now up to you: your income, your schedule, your results. The freedom you crave won't be immediate or total. In fact, you may work more hours at first than at your current job, because building something from scratch isn't a 9-to-5 job, it's a constant commitment. But that freedom, if you're willing to pay the initial price, is real and worth it.

It's important to take a moment to reflect on your values and priorities. What's most important to you? Maybe it's spending more time with your family, dedicating yourself to a project that has a positive impact on the world, or simply proving to yourself that you're capable of creating something with your own hands. Identifying these priorities will help you align your business decisions with what really matters to you, preventing you from getting lost along the way chasing goals that don't fulfill you.

It is also valid to recognize that fear can be part of your motivation. The fear of staying in the same place, of the years passing without significant changes, or of reaching the end of your life wondering what would have happened if you had dared. That fear, well channeled, can be a powerful driving force. It is not about starting a business to escape from something, but for the excitement of building something new.

Finally, remember that there is no single correct reason to start a business. It can be a combination of factors: a passion that you want to turn into a business, the desire for a brighter future, or simply the need for a change. The important thing is that you are clear about your reasons and that they are strong enough to sustain you when things don't go as you expected. Because starting a business is not an easy path, but when you do it with purpose, every challenge becomes an opportunity to grow and get closer to that life you always dreamed of.

Self-Knowledge and Transferable Skills

Self-awareness is one of the most valuable tools you can develop when starting out on the path of entrepreneurship. Knowing who you are, what skills you have, and how these can help you build a solid business is essential to making smart decisions. Before you worry about business models or marketing strategies, you need to look in the mirror and be completely honest with yourself. This step may seem simple, but many people overlook it, and the result is that they end up choosing a venture they are not passionate about or ready for.

Let's start with the basics: what are you good at? People often underestimate their own skills because they see them as too simple or of little value. Maybe you're great at organizing events, explaining complicated concepts in a simple way, or solving technical problems. Maybe you have a knack for connecting with people, negotiating, or finding creative solutions to challenges. These are your transferable skills, and even if you use them in a specific work context right now, they can be applied to your own business if you know how to recognize them.

To identify these skills, think about what you do in your current job or your everyday activities that others find difficult but that come naturally to you. For example, if you are responsible for coordinating teams in your current job, that skill may transfer to managing a team within your business. If you enjoy designing or creating things, there may be an opportunity for you to pursue a career in a creative field. Even if what you are passionate about seems unrelated to your work experience, there are ways to connect the dots.

The next step is to recognize your areas for improvement. This doesn't mean focusing on your weaknesses to discourage yourself, but rather to understand what aspects you will need to strengthen or delegate. For example, if you have great ideas but you're not good with numbers, it's important to know this from the beginning in order to seek support from someone who can cover that part. Entrepreneurship doesn't mean you have to do everything alone; it's about using your skills to the fullest and building a team or system that compensates for what you lack.

In addition to analyzing your skills, it's important to reflect on your personality. Are you a person who is comfortable taking risks, or do you prefer a safer approach? Do you enjoy constant interactions with others, or do you find it more natural to work independently? Knowing these characteristics will help you choose a business model that aligns with your personality. For example, someone who is extroverted may feel more comfortable in a business that involves public relations or direct sales, while someone who is introverted may prefer an e-commerce model or a business based on digital content.

Another key aspect of self-awareness is identifying your values and motivations. What really matters to you? Is it financial freedom, flexible hours, or the opportunity to do something meaningful? Your values will be the compass that guides you through important decisions, from what type of business to choose to how to run it. If your values are not aligned with your venture, you are likely to feel frustrated or dissatisfied, even if the business is financially successful.

Once you have clarity about your skills and personality, the next step is to look for ways to apply what you know to the world of entrepreneurship. For example, if you have learned how to solve problems under pressure in your current job, that same skill will be crucial to dealing with challenges that arise in your business. If you have experience in customer service, you will be able to use that foundation to build strong relationships with your future clients. Everything you have learned so far, even what you consider less important, can be useful if you know how to adapt it.

It's also important to understand that self-knowledge is an ongoing process. It's not about sitting down one day to write a list of your skills and then forgetting about it. As you progress along your entrepreneurial path, you'll discover new strengths and, probably, new challenges. The important thing is to keep an open mind and be willing to learn from each experience.

Self-awareness and the recognition of your transferable skills not only prepare you for entrepreneurship, but also give you confidence. Knowing who you are and what you can offer the world is a huge advantage in a competitive market. In the end, the most successful businesses don't just solve problems or satisfy needs; they also reflect the authenticity and strengths of those who lead them. That connection between your essence and your business will be what sets you apart and drives you towards success.

Entrepreneur Mindset

To go from being an employee to becoming an entrepreneur, the first change is not in your job or your bank account. It's in your mind. Changing your mindset is perhaps the hardest step, but also the most important. The way you think defines how you act and how you face challenges. If you continue to think like an employee, even when running your own business, it will be difficult for you to achieve success. So, how do you think like an entrepreneur? The answer is not a secret, but it is a process that requires commitment and constant effort.

The first shift you need to make is to stop thinking in terms of security and start thinking in terms of possibilities. As an employee, your job is to fulfill a list of specific responsibilities, in exchange for a steady paycheck. That stability can be comfortable, but it's also a comfort zone that limits your growth. An entrepreneur, on the other hand, doesn't have a guaranteed paycheck at the end of the month. What they do have is the ability to create value and generate income based on the opportunities they identify and take advantage of. To be an entrepreneur, you need to get used to the idea that risk and uncertainty are part of the journey, but so is freedom and unlimited potential.

Another key aspect of the entrepreneurial mindset is learning how to make decisions. As an employee, many important decisions are likely to be made by your bosses or the organization. In your business, all decisions will fall to you. Some will be small, like choosing a design for your logo, and others will be gigantic, like investing in a project that could change the course of your company. The key is to accept that you will never have all the information you want before you decide, but you can't be paralyzed. Successful entrepreneurs make decisions with the best information available at the time, and they learn from the consequences, whether good or bad.

Thinking like an entrepreneur also involves developing a long-term vision. As an employee, your focus may be on meeting this month's goals or on the next paycheck. But an entrepreneur always has one eye on the future. Where do you want your business to be in five or ten years? What steps do you need to take today to get closer to that goal?

Having a clear vision will not only help you make better decisions, but it will also give you the motivation to keep going when you face challenges.

Resilience is another key element. As an employee, you may be used to receiving clear instructions and following established processes. But in the world of entrepreneurship, there won't always be a manual telling you what to do. There will be days when you feel like nothing is working, and other days when your efforts seem to be going nowhere. It's at these times that an entrepreneurial mindset makes all the difference. An entrepreneur doesn't give up at the first hurdle. Instead of seeing problems as failures, he sees them as lessons that bring him closer to his goal.

Another crucial aspect is changing your relationship with money. As an employee, money can be seen as a limited resource that you receive in exchange for hours worked. But as an entrepreneur, money is a tool that you can use to create more value. This means you will have to learn how to reinvest in your business, spend wisely, and manage cash flow. It also means you must overcome your fear of investing. The money you invest in your business is not an expense, it is a bet on yourself and your ability to create something worthwhile.

The entrepreneurial mindset also includes accepting that learning never ends. As an employee, it's common to specialize in one area and stay there. But an entrepreneur must be a constant learner. You may need to learn about marketing, sales, technology, or even basic negotiation skills. The key is to always be willing to expand your knowledge and skills, because the business world is constantly changing, and only those who are prepared to adapt survive and thrive.

Finally, think about the impact you want to have. An entrepreneur doesn't just want to make money, but also to create something that leaves a mark. Whether it's a product that makes people's lives easier, a service that solves a problem, or even a business that inspires others to follow their dreams. Having a clear purpose and a positive impact will not only make you happier, but will also attract customers, employees, and partners who share your values and vision.

Changing your mindset isn't something that happens overnight. It takes daily practice, reflection, and sometimes uncomfortable moments where you challenge yourself. But once you get the hang of thinking like an entrepreneur, you won't just own your business; you'll own your life and your future. And that's the true reward of entrepreneurship.

Choosing the Ideal Entrepreneurship

Choosing the ideal venture can be one of the most exciting and challenging decisions on the road to becoming an entrepreneur. It's not just about looking for something that is profitable, but also about finding an idea that is aligned with your skills, interests, and goals. The business you choose will be an important part of your life, so you shouldn't make this decision lightly. The key is to balance passion with strategy. That is, something that you are passionate about, but that also has a market willing to pay for it.

The first step is to introspect about what really motivates you. What is it that you enjoy doing even when no one asks you to? Maybe you love cooking, writing, teaching, or working with technology. That passion can be a major clue. If you choose a business in an area you don't like, you'll have a hard time staying motivated in the long run. However, passion alone isn't enough. You should also ask yourself if you have any skills or knowledge that give you an edge in that area. For example, if you love cooking but don't know anything about management, maybe you need to do some preparation before opening a restaurant.

Once you have a list of things you're interested in, it's time to analyze the market. Passion without a market is just a hobby, not a business. Ask yourself: Are there people willing to pay for what I plan to offer? Who would be my customers? What problems would my product or service solve? This requires research. You can start by searching the internet, talking to potential customers, or even analyzing what your future competitors are doing. The idea is not to copy, but to understand what works in the market and what you can offer differently.

It's also important to consider the business model. A business model is basically the way your idea is going to generate revenue. Some models require a significant initial investment, such as opening a brick-and-mortar store or restaurant. Others can start with few resources, such as an online business or consulting services. If your finances are limited, it's best to opt for a model that doesn't require large investments at the beginning. This will allow you to minimize risks while testing your idea.

Financial viability is another critical factor. It doesn't matter how passionate you are about an idea if it isn't financially sustainable. You need to figure out how much it will cost to start and operate the business, and how long you think it will take before it starts generating profits. Make your numbers realistic. Many businesses fail because entrepreneurs underestimate costs or overestimate profits. Make sure you have a clear plan to cover initial expenses, whether through savings, financing, or a side income while the business takes off.

In addition to feasibility, consider the time and effort you're willing to invest. Not all businesses require the same level of commitment. For example, selling products online can be more flexible in terms of schedule than running a brick-and-mortar store, where you must be present all the time. If you have other responsibilities, such as a current job or a family, consider how the business will fit into your lifestyle. Choosing something that aligns with your personal priorities will make the process much more bearable.

Another key part is analyzing risks. Every business has risks, but some are more manageable than others. For example, a service-based business may require less initial investment and therefore less financial risk. In contrast, a business that involves manufacturing a product may require significant investment in inventory or machinery. Evaluate how much risk you are willing to take and plan how to minimize it. This doesn't mean avoiding risks altogether, but being smart about facing them.

A common mistake when choosing a venture is trying to do it all alone. Don't underestimate the importance of seeking support and opinions. Talk to trusted people, mentors, or even other entrepreneurs. Their perspectives can help you identify strengths or weaknesses in your idea. Also, consider whether the business you have in mind can be run alone or if you'll need to build a team. Some ideas may be too complex for one person, and it's okay to seek help early on.

Finally, imagine what your life would be like if this business is successful. Do you see yourself happy running it on a daily basis? Is it something you could do for years without feeling burned out or dissatisfied? The ideal idea should not only work on paper, but also in practice. Visualize how it will fit into your life and whether it will allow you to achieve the goals that really matter to you, such as financial freedom, time flexibility, or the impact you want to have on the world.

Choosing the ideal business venture is not a decision you should make overnight. It is a process that requires reflection, research, and above all, honesty with yourself. There is no one-size-fits-all formula, but if you take the time to analyze your passions, skills, and the market, you will be much closer to finding an idea that is not only profitable, but also makes you happy. Remember that a successful business is one that not only makes money, but also becomes an extension of who you are and what you truly value.

Assessing Risks and Defining Strategies

On the road to entrepreneurship, one of the most important tasks is to assess the risks and define strategies to deal with them. The mistake many entrepreneurs make is to jump into the water without considering the possible obstacles. Although you can't eliminate all risks, you can reduce them and be prepared to handle them effectively. Assessing risks doesn't mean being pessimistic; it means being realistic and having a solid plan for the unexpected.

The first step in assessing risks is to identify which risks are most common in the type of business you plan to start. For example, if you want to open a restaurant, some risks might be high operating costs, staff turnover, or variability in customer demand. If you plan to sell products online, risks might include inventory issues, intense competition, or difficulty attracting traffic to your website. Every business model has its own challenges, so you should spend time researching and understanding the specifics of your industry.

Once you've identified potential risks, rank them based on their likelihood of occurrence and their impact. For example, a risk with a high probability and high impact, such as a lack of customers during the first few months, should be prioritized in your strategy. On the other hand, an unlikely and low-impact risk, such as a small delay in a delivery, can be monitored without needing to invest too many resources in resolving it beforehand. This approach will help you focus your energy on what really matters.

After you've identified and categorized risks, it's time to define strategies to manage them. These strategies can be divided into four categories: prevent, reduce, transfer, and accept. Prevent involves taking steps to prevent the risk from occurring in the first place. For example, if you're worried about not attracting enough customers, you might invest in a solid marketing strategy before launching your business. Reduce means minimizing the impact of the risk if it occurs. If you're afraid of running out of money, you might set up an emergency fund or seek additional financing. Transfer involves delegating the risk to another party, such as purchasing insurance to protect your inventory. Finally, accept means recognizing that some risks are inevitable and being prepared to deal with them when they arise.

It's important that these strategies are specific and practical. Saying that you will "prepare for whatever comes next" is not enough. If you have identified that one of your concerns is competition, a concrete strategy could be to analyze your competitors' prices and offers regularly to stay competitive. If one of your risks is a lack of experience in finance, you could plan to take a basic course or hire an accountant. The more detailed and realistic your strategies are, the more confident you will be moving forward.

A common mistake when assessing risks is to focus only on the negative aspects. Sure, the goal is to protect your business, but you can also identify opportunities while analyzing risks. For example, if you discover that there are many competitors in your market, that risk may also indicate that there is high demand. If you anticipate that initial costs will be high, you may be able to negotiate with suppliers to reduce them.

Approaching risks with an open mind can help you discover innovative solutions.

In addition to strategies, it is essential to create an action plan in case the risks become a reality. This plan should include clear steps on what to do, who will be responsible, and how to minimize the damage. For example, if you run an online business and experience a drop in sales, your plan could include analyzing your website traffic data, reviewing your advertising campaigns, and adjusting your marketing strategy. Having a plan will give you peace of mind and allow you to act quickly instead of panicking.

Remember that not all risks can be anticipated. That's why it's important to remain flexible and willing to adapt. Resilience is one of the most important characteristics of a good entrepreneur. There will be times when, despite your best efforts, things won't go as you expected. But if you're prepared to learn from setbacks and adjust your strategy, you'll be able to keep moving forward.

Finally, assess risks regularly, even after your business is up and running. The business environment is constantly changing, and what was a low risk a year ago could become a serious threat. Set up a system to review risks periodically, either quarterly or whenever significant changes occur in your industry. This habit will not only protect your business, but it will also allow you to identify new opportunities.

Assessing risks and defining strategies is not an exciting step, but it is one of the most important steps to ensure the success of your venture. This process will allow you to build a stronger business, reduce stress, and be better prepared for any challenges that may arise. With careful planning, you will be one step closer to turning your ideas into a successful reality.

Building a Transition Fund

When you decide to make the jump from employee to entrepreneur, one of the biggest hurdles is financial uncertainty. Switching from a stable, predictable income to the fluctuating income that comes with entrepreneurship can be scary. That's why building a transition fund is critical. Not only will this fund give you peace of mind, but it will also allow you to focus on your business without constantly worrying about how you'll pay your bills.

A bridging fund is basically a savings plan designed to cover your basic expenses while your business gets off the ground. The first question you need to ask yourself is: how much money do I need to live on each month? This includes your fixed expenses, such as rent or mortgage, utilities, transportation, and food, but also other variable costs such as entertainment, insurance, and debt. It's critical to be honest with yourself in this analysis. If you underestimate your expenses, you could find yourself short at the worst possible time.

Once you're clear on how much you need on a monthly basis, the next step is to figure out how long you expect it to take before your business generates steady revenue. For some businesses, this might be three to six months. For others, it could take a year or more. If you're unsure, it's best to be conservative and plan for a longer period. For example, if you need $2,000 a month and you estimate it will take six months for your business to become stable, your transition fund should be at least $12,000.

The next step is to establish a strategy for building this fund. If you're currently working, use your salary as a starting point. Assess your expenses and look for areas where you can cut back to save faster. Maybe you can cut back on restaurant outings, postpone large purchases, or cancel subscriptions you don't use. Every little adjustment counts, and the temporary sacrifice will be worth it when you have a financial cushion that allows you to confidently take action.

In addition to cutting expenses, consider how you can increase your income while building your fund. This could include taking on a side job, selling items you no longer need, or pursuing freelance projects related to the skills you plan to use in your business. Even a few extra hours of work a week can make a big difference over several months.

While you're saving, make sure you keep the money in a separate account. This will help keep it out of reach for everyday expenses and allow you to clearly see your progress. An interest-bearing savings account can be a good option, as it will allow you to earn a little extra while you build up your fund. However, avoid risky or long-term investments, as you need this money to be available when you need it.

It's important to understand that this fund benefits not only you, but your business as well. When you have a financial cushion, you can make calm and strategic business decisions instead of acting out of desperation. For example, if you need to invest in marketing or purchase essential tools, you can do so without worrying about running out of money to pay rent.

Some people hesitate to save for a transition fund because they feel like they're delaying their entrepreneurial dream. But this step isn't a delay, it's an investment in your success. By building this fund, you're giving yourself the gift of time and stability to fully focus on your business when the time comes. Without this foundation, you could find yourself in a situation where you have to abandon your project due to lack of resources before it has a chance to get off the ground.

In addition to saving, consider how you can structure your personal and business finances to minimize risk. If possible, keep your current job while you begin working on your business idea part-time. Not only will this allow you to save faster, but it will also give you the opportunity to test your idea in the market without risking everything from the start.

Once you have your fund in place and decide to make the transition, use it wisely. This money is not for luxuries or unnecessary expenses. It is a resource designed to cover the essentials while you build your business. Try to stretch it as much as you can, looking for ways to cut costs in both your personal life and your business. For example, you could work from home instead of renting an office or look for cheaper suppliers for your inputs.

Finally, remember that the transition fund is not only a financial tool, but also an emotional one. Knowing that you have a backup will allow you to face the challenges of entrepreneurship with more confidence and less stress. When you are not worried about how you will pay your bills, you can focus on what really matters: building a solid and sustainable business.

Creating a transition fund requires discipline, patience, and planning. But by doing so, you will be taking one of the smartest and most responsible steps toward your goal of becoming an entrepreneur. It is an endeavor that will give you the freedom and security to pursue your dreams without compromising your financial stability or your peace of mind. And that peace of mind will be your greatest ally on the road to success.

Time, Money and Energy

One of the biggest challenges when transitioning from employee to entrepreneur is learning how to manage your most valuable resources: time, money, and energy. These three elements are deeply connected, and if not managed carefully, they can become obstacles rather than tools for success. The good news is that with planning and discipline, you can use them efficiently to build a solid business without compromising your personal well-being.

Time is a limited resource, but we often treat it as if it were infinite. When you work as an employee, your schedule is often structured by others. However, as an entrepreneur, you have to learn to be your own boss and decide how to spend your hours. This can be exciting, but it's also a double-edged sword. Without good time management, it's easy to fall into the trap of being busy without being productive. So before you get started, it's important to ask yourself one crucial question: what am I currently spending my time on?

Take an honest look at how you spend your days. Jot down how much time you spend working, sleeping, socializing, exercising, and doing leisure activities. This will give you a clear picture of where you could adjust to free up hours for your business. You might find that you spend too much time on social media or watching TV. These hours can be redirected toward more productive tasks, such as planning your business, learning new skills, or working on your startup idea.

The next step is to set clear priorities. Not all tasks have the same level of importance, and it is essential that you learn to differentiate between what is urgent and what is important. For example, answering emails may seem urgent, but developing a solid business plan is much more important for long-term success. Use tools such as to-do lists, calendars, and time management techniques, such as the Pomodoro technique, to stay focused and organized.

Money is another essential resource that needs to be managed wisely. In the beginning, your income is likely to be unstable, so every expense should be carefully evaluated. Before you set out, make a detailed budget of your personal and business finances. This includes your current income, your monthly expenses, and any debt you have. Knowing exactly how much you need to cover your basic needs will help you avoid financial stress during the first few months of your business.

Additionally, you need to be realistic about the costs of starting and operating your business. Research how much it will cost to produce your product or service, market it, and keep it running. If you find that you need more money than you have available, consider options to increase your income before quitting your current job. This could include finding temporary side work, selling assets you don't need, or exploring outside financing, such as loans or investors.

However, be careful not to fall into the trap of spending money on unnecessary things at the beginning. It's easy to get excited about having a fancy office, the latest technological equipment or an expensive advertising campaign. But at this stage, the most important thing is to keep costs low and focus on the essentials. Remember that every dollar you save now is a dollar you can reinvest in your business later.

Energy is the third key resource and often the most underrated. It doesn't matter how much time and money you have if you don't have the energy to use them effectively. Being an entrepreneur requires a level of mental, physical and emotional effort that can be exhausting if you don't take care of yourself. That's why it's critical that you learn to manage your energy wisely.

Start by taking care of your physical health. A balanced diet, regular exercise, and good sleep aren't just wellness tips; they're essential tools for keeping your energy at its peak. When you're physically fit, you can work longer hours without feeling exhausted and make clearer, more rational decisions.

In addition to physical health, pay attention to your mental health. Stress and anxiety are frequent companions on the entrepreneurial journey, but you can manage them through practices like meditation, journaling, or simply taking time to unplug. Surround yourself with supportive and inspiring people, and don't hesitate to seek professional help if you feel overwhelmed.

Finally, learn to recognize your energy peaks and valleys throughout the day. Some people are most productive in the morning, while others prefer to work in the afternoon or evening. Identify when you feel most focused and use that time to accomplish the most important and demanding tasks. Leave the more routine tasks, such as answering emails or making calls, for times when your energy is lowest.

Balancing time, money and energy is crucial. If you focus solely on one of these resources and neglect the others, your progress will suffer. For example, working too many hours to save money can lead to burnout, while spending too much money to save time could put your financial stability at risk.

The key is to understand that these resources are interdependent. Time allows you to make money, money allows you to optimize your time, and energy is what makes both useful. When you learn to manage these three resources effectively, you create a solid foundation for success not only in your business, but in your personal life as well.

Managing your time, money, and energy isn't a one-time thing. It's an ongoing process that requires constant adjustments. As your business grows and your circumstances change, you'll need to reevaluate your priorities and strategies. But if you start with a solid foundation and a conscious mindset, you'll be much better prepared to meet the challenges of entrepreneurship and build the business you dream of.

The Power of Plan B

Entrepreneurship is an act of courage and vision, but it also means accepting a considerable dose of uncertainty. No matter how prepared you are or how much you have planned, there will always be factors that are beyond your control. An unexpected economic downturn, a change in market trends, or even personal problems can throw you off course. That's why having a plan B is not just an option, it's a necessity. Plan B doesn't mean you don't trust your main idea, but rather that you understand that life is unpredictable and that being prepared for the unexpected can make the difference between overcoming an obstacle or staying stuck.

The first step in developing a Plan B is to accept that things won't always go the way you imagined. This isn't pessimism, it's pragmatism. Recognizing that setbacks can arise will allow you to approach them with a strategic mindset rather than reacting impulsively. A Plan B isn't a sign of weakness, it's a sign of intelligence. The most successful entrepreneurs in the world don't blindly cling to a single idea; they're constantly thinking about how to adapt if things don't go the way they expected.

A well-designed Plan B starts with an honest assessment of your business and your finances. Ask yourself how critical the immediate success of your main idea is to your stability. For example, if your business doesn't generate revenue in the first few months, what alternatives do you have to stay afloat? Perhaps you can continue working part-time at your current job, offer freelance services related to your skills, or even look for partners who can provide additional resources.

Plan B should also consider scenarios where you need to adjust your business model. For example, if you are selling a product and sales are not meeting your expectations, you could pivot to a service-based model or find a different market where your product is more in demand. This isn't about abandoning your vision, but rather finding an alternative way to keep it alive. This kind of flexibility can be the difference between closing your business or finding a new opportunity within an apparent crisis.

It's important to note that a plan B is not the same as a defeatist mindset. Having a backup plan doesn't mean you don't trust your plan A, but that you're prepared to face any challenge. In fact, having a plan B can give you more confidence to pursue your main idea, because you know you have a safety net if something doesn't work out the way you expected.

In addition to a backup plan for your business, you also need a backup plan for your personal life. What will you do if your business takes longer than expected to generate revenue? How will you manage your expenses and responsibilities? Consider creating an emergency fund that will cover your basic needs for an additional period of time. This fund can be an extension of your transition fund or a completely separate reserve, but it will give you peace of mind as you navigate the ups and downs of entrepreneurship.

Another crucial aspect of Plan B is the ability to temporarily return to a job if things don't go as you hoped. This shouldn't be seen as a failure, but rather as a smart strategy to regroup and try again from a stronger position. Many people fear that returning to a job will be a setback, but in reality, it can be a way to recharge your resources, learn new skills, and return to the path of entrepreneurship with more experience and confidence.

Your Plan B can also include strategic alliances. If your business is facing difficulties, you may be able to collaborate with other entrepreneurs or companies to share resources and expand your opportunities. Partnerships can open doors you hadn't considered and offer new ways to generate income or diversify your business model.

It's critical that your Plan B is specific and realistic. It's not enough to just say you have a backup plan—you need to know exactly what you'll do, when you'll do it, and how you'll implement it. For example, if your Plan B involves looking for temporary employment, have a list of industries or companies you could approach. If you plan to change your business model, define what products or services you'd offer and how you'd promote them. The more detailed your plan is, the more prepared you'll be to activate it if necessary.

Finally, review and update your plan B regularly. As your business grows, market conditions change, or your personal circumstances evolve, your backup plan should adapt as well. What seemed like a good solution a year ago may not be relevant now, so take the time to re-evaluate your options and make sure your plan B is still viable.

Having a plan B doesn't mean you expect to fail, it means you're willing to do whatever it takes to succeed. It's a reminder that resilience and adaptability are essential on the path of entrepreneurship. When you have a plan B, no matter how tough things get, you'll always have a way to keep moving forward. And that's one of the greatest strengths you can have as an entrepreneur.

Validating Your Business Idea

Before you commit time, money, and energy to your business idea, it's crucial to validate that it has the potential to become profitable. Validation not only saves you resources, but it also gives you the confidence to move forward with confidence. In simple terms, validating a business idea means confirming that there are people willing to pay for what you offer and that your solution meets a real need. This step is essential to avoid falling into the trap of building something that no one wants.

The validation process starts with a key question: who are you helping and what problem are you solving? Your business idea should focus on a specific problem that affects a group of people. This problem can be something big and obvious, like the need for affordable transportation, or something small but important, like a handy accessory for organizing cables. The important thing is that your solution is relevant and provides value.

Once you've identified the problem, clearly define your target audience. Think about who are the people who are most likely to need what you offer. Don't try to be all-encompassing, because that dilutes your message and makes it harder to connect with your potential customers. For example, if you're developing a productivity app, is it targeted at students, busy professionals, or entrepreneurs? The more specific you are in defining your audience, the easier it will be to tailor your idea to their needs.

With your target audience in mind, it's time to investigate whether the problem you've identified actually matters to them. This is where many business ideas fail, because entrepreneurs assume they know their audience's needs without confirming whether they're real. To avoid this, talk directly to the people you want to help. Conduct interviews, surveys, or even informal Q&A sessions. Ask what challenges they face, how they currently try to solve them, and what they'd be willing to pay for a better solution.

Don't just ask if they like your idea. It's easy for people to say something sounds good just to be nice, but that doesn't mean they'd buy it. Instead, look for signs of real commitment. For example, if they mention they're already spending money on similar solutions, that's a good sign your idea has potential. Conversely, if they're not willing to spend money or time solving the problem, your idea may not be as viable as you thought.

Another powerful tool to validate your idea is to create a prototype or minimum viable version of your product or service. This doesn't have to be something fully developed, but rather a basic representation that allows people to interact with your solution. For example, if you plan to open a food business, you could offer samples at local events to get feedback. If you're developing an app, you could create a simple demo that shows off the main features. The goal is to test your idea with as little investment as possible to see if it resonates with your target audience.

Once you have your prototype ready, test your idea in a real-world environment. This may mean selling your product to a small group of people, offering free services in exchange for honest feedback, or launching a pre-sale campaign to gauge interest. The key is to observe how people react when they have the opportunity to use or buy your solution. If you get positive results, such as initial sales, good feedback, or recommendations, that indicates that your idea has a market.

While you're validating your idea, it's also important to look at your competitors. They can be a valuable source of information about what works and what doesn't. Analyze how they solve the problem you also want to address, what prices they charge, and how they reach their customers. This doesn't mean you should copy what they do, but you should learn from their successes and mistakes to perfect your own proposition.

Validation doesn't end with the first positive results. Once you confirm that your idea has potential, keep looking for ways to improve it. Customer needs can change, and what works today may not be as effective in the future. Stay in touch with your audience, continue collecting feedback, and adapt your business according to new opportunities and challenges that arise.

It's important to remember that not every idea will make it through the validation process, and that's okay. If you find that your idea isn't viable, don't view it as a failure, but rather as an opportunity to adjust your approach or explore new possibilities. Entrepreneurship is a continuous learning process, and every step, even the ones that don't go as you expected, brings you closer to your goal.

Validating your business idea is not a luxury, it is a necessity. Although it may be tempting to skip this step in order to get started as soon as possible, investing time in confirming that your idea has potential will save you a lot of trouble in the future. It is a process that allows you to move forward with confidence, knowing that you are building something that can really succeed. When you are clear about the value of your idea and the impact it can have on people's lives, you become not only an entrepreneur, but someone who brings real solutions to the world.

Learning from Others

On the road to becoming an entrepreneur, one of the most valuable tools you can use is the experience of others. Whether you're starting from scratch or already have some experience, there's always someone who has faced similar challenges to yours and found ways to overcome them. Learning from others not only saves you time and effort, but it also gives you perspectives you might never have considered on your own. This approach isn't a shortcut—it's a smart strategy for moving forward with fewer setbacks.

The first step to learning from others is to identify who you can observe or gain knowledge from. These can be successful entrepreneurs in your industry, mentors, colleagues, or even people who have failed at their ventures. Each of these experiences has something to teach you. For example, a successful entrepreneur can show you how to build a solid business, while someone who failed at their goal can help you avoid costly mistakes.

To learn from others effectively, don't be afraid to seek advice directly. Many people are willing to share their knowledge if you ask them humbly and with a genuine interest in learning. This could mean sending an email, attending networking events, or even reaching out through social media. When you reach out, be specific about what you want to know. Instead of asking for a generic chat, ask something concrete, like how they managed to overcome a particular obstacle or what strategies worked best for them when starting out.

An effective way to learn is through books, podcasts, and interviews of entrepreneurs. We live in an era where knowledge is at our fingertips. There are books written by entrepreneurs sharing their successes, failures, and most important learnings. Podcasts, on the other hand, are an accessible and free way to listen to conversations with industry leaders and experts. Even a single piece of advice heard at the right time can make a huge difference in your journey as an entrepreneur.

Also, never underestimate the power of communities. Local entrepreneur groups, online forums, and business associations are great places to connect with people who are on the same path as you. These communities are not only sources of inspiration, but also support. Here you can share your ideas, receive feedback, and learn from others' experiences in real time. For example, if you're facing a problem with your business's marketing, chances are someone in your community has been there and can offer a practical solution.

Another powerful way to learn is by observing how other businesses operate, even if you don't have direct access to their founders. Analyze their marketing strategies, their business models, and how they interact with their customers. If they have a product or service that competes with yours, think about what they're doing well and how you can differentiate yourself. If they don't compete directly, try to identify best practices that you can adapt to your own venture.

If you have the opportunity, consider finding a mentor. A mentor is someone with experience who can guide you and help you make more informed decisions. Mentors not only offer practical advice, but they can also help keep you motivated when things get tough. Find someone who is aligned with your goals and understands the challenges of your industry. Having someone who has already walked the path can be one of the best investments you make in your personal and professional development.

It's also important to learn from others' failures, not just their successes. Failure is an inevitable part of entrepreneurship, and many successful entrepreneurs have had to overcome major setbacks before getting to where they are. Research stories of businesses that didn't work out and reflect on what went wrong. Was there a lack of validation of the idea? Was there poor financial management? Learning from these cases can help you anticipate problems and prepare strategies to avoid them.

Also, don't limit your learning to people within your industry. The most innovative ideas often come from combining approaches from different fields. For example, an entrepreneur in technology can learn from the hospitality industry's customer service strategies. Keep an open mind and look for inspiration in unexpected places.

Finally, remember that learning from others is not something you do once, but rather a constant habit. There will always be something new to discover and ways to improve. Make learning a central part of your life as an entrepreneur. Read, listen, observe, and ask questions. Every experience, whether someone else's or your own, has the potential to teach you something valuable.

The path of entrepreneurship is much more rewarding when you walk it accompanied by the lessons of those who have come before you. Taking advantage of that knowledge not only better prepares you for challenges, but also gives you a competitive advantage. Learning from others does not make you a copycat, it makes you wiser and more prepared. It is a powerful tool that, when used correctly, can be the engine that drives you to success.

When is the Right Time to Quit

Deciding when the right time is to quit your job can be one of the most difficult steps on the path to becoming an entrepreneur. It is not a decision you should take lightly, because it means leaving behind the security of a steady income and the structure that a conventional job provides. However, it is also a necessary step in order to fully dedicate yourself to your venture. The key is to make this transition strategically, calculatedly, and at the right time to minimize risks and maximize your chances of success.

The first sign that you might be ready to call it quits is when your business shows clear signs of viability. This means you've validated your idea, you've started generating consistent revenue, and you have a clear plan for how to scale. If your venture hasn't reached this point yet, quitting may be a mistake, because you'll be relying on something that isn't solid enough yet. Make sure your business not only has potential, but also has a stable foundation that can sustain your basic financial needs.

Another important factor to consider is your emergency fund. Before you leave your job, you need to have enough money saved to cover at least six months of your essential expenses. This includes rent or mortgage, food, transportation, insurance, and any other financial obligations. This fund is non-negotiable, because it will give you peace of mind and wiggle room while you work on growing your business. If you don't have this financial cushion, it may be better to wait and keep working while you build it.

Your level of commitment also plays a crucial role. Ask yourself if you're ready to dedicate all your time, energy, and resources to your venture. Being an entrepreneur isn't easy, and while many people dream of the independence it offers, the reality is that it requires a great deal of hard work, especially in the beginning. If you still have doubts or feel unsure about your capabilities, you may need more time to prepare yourself before taking this leap.

Evaluate how your current job is affecting your business, too. If your current job is starting to seriously interfere with your ability to grow your business, this could be a sign that it's time to quit. For example, if you're constantly feeling burned out, don't have time to serve clients, or can't meet important deadlines, it can be difficult to move your business forward while maintaining a full-time job. However, if you can still manage both without compromising either too much, consider staying at your job a little longer.

Talk to your support network before making the final decision. This includes your family, partner, or anyone who depends on you or shares your financial responsibilities. Explain your plans, your reasons, and how you plan to handle the transition. Their opinions can not only offer you new perspectives, but can also help you identify areas you may not have considered. Open and honest communication with those closest to you is essential to ensure everyone is aligned with your decision.

Another aspect to consider is planning a strategic exit. Quitting your job shouldn't be a knee-jerk reaction. Find out about your company's policies, such as notice periods, and plan your resignation in a professional manner. Not only will this help you maintain a good relationship with your employer, but it can also open the door to future opportunities, such as referrals or even collaborations with your business.

If you're still unsure, consider trying a gradual approach. This could mean reducing your work hours or negotiating a flexible schedule that allows you to devote more time to your venture. While this option isn't always possible, many people find that a transition period gives them the confidence and resources they need to make the full leap later on.

Remember that there is no perfect time to quit. There will always be uncertainty and risk involved in this decision, but the important thing is to minimize those risks as much as possible. If you wait until everything is absolutely certain, you will likely never take the step. Instead, focus on preparing everything necessary to make your transition as smooth as possible.

Lastly, trust yourself. If you've done the work necessary to validate your business, build an emergency fund, and mentally prepare yourself for challenges, then you're likely ready to take the next step. Fear will always be there, but don't let it paralyze you. Making the decision to quit your job to follow your dreams is one of the bravest things you can do. Make sure you do it smartly, but also with the conviction that you're choosing a path that can change your life forever.

Negotiation and Graceful Exit from Work

Quitting your job doesn't mean simply handing in a resignation letter and walking out the door. A well-planned and graceful exit can make a huge difference to your professional reputation, your relationship with former colleagues, and future opportunities. How you handle your exit will say a lot about you as a professional and as a person. It's an opportunity to close this chapter of your work life with integrity, gratitude, and professionalism.

The first step to a graceful exit is to be honest with yourself about your reasons for leaving. When you decide to take a career, it's common to feel excited about your future, but you should also be aware that your decision may generate reactions at your workplace. You don't have to share every detail, but it's important to prepare a clear and respectful explanation of your reasons. You can mention that you're exploring new opportunities, seeking personal growth, or pursuing a dream, without needing to get too specific.

It's essential to comply with the advance notice period that your contract requires or that is considered standard in your industry. Typically, this period ranges from two weeks to a month, but be sure to check your company's specific policies. Complying with this requirement is not only an act of courtesy, but also shows respect for your employer and your coworkers, who will have to adjust to your departure.

When communicating your decision to your boss, do so in person if possible. Ask for a private meeting and make sure the timing is right. During the conversation, be direct but also respectful. Express gratitude for the opportunities your job has provided and emphasize that you value all you have learned. A grateful attitude can help soften the news and leave a positive impression.

Prepare a professional resignation letter. This document should be brief, direct, and focused on the facts. Include the date you plan to leave the position and a brief thank you for the opportunity to work for the company. It is not necessary to go into detail about your future plans, especially if you are starting a business that could be perceived as competition. Keep the tone of the letter neutral and professional.

It's equally important to be a team player during your final weeks at the company. Don't slow down or neglect your responsibilities. Help train your replacement, document important processes, and offer assistance to make the transition as smooth as possible. Your colleagues will remember how you performed during this period, and a good impression can open doors for you in the future.

If you have a positive relationship with your boss and colleagues, this may also be a good time to ask for references. Do so in a polite, non-pressured manner. Explain that you value their opinion and that it would be meaningful to you to have their support in your future endeavors. Even if you don't need references right away, having people willing to back you up is a valuable asset.

Also, keep your future plans confidential, especially if you are starting a business in a sector related to your current job. Talking too much about your venture can lead to misunderstandings or even unnecessary tensions. The best strategy is to maintain a professional approach, focusing on being grateful and closing your career in the best possible way.

You should also prepare for potential negotiations. In some cases, your employer might offer you a counteroffer to stay. This may include a raise, a promotion, or additional benefits. If this happens, listen carefully to the proposal, but stay true to your goals. Remember why you decided to start your career and consider whether accepting a counteroffer really aligns with your long-term goals. Don't let a momentary attractive offer distract you from what you really want.

When your last day comes, take the opportunity to say goodbye in a personal way. A farewell email is a great way to thank your colleagues for their support and wish them the best in the future. Keep the message short, positive and professional. Include your contact details if you wish to stay in touch with them. Never underestimate the importance of these relationships, as they could be valuable to you in the future.

Finally, remember that a graceful exit doesn't end the day you hand over your computer and say goodbye. Maintain a professional attitude even after you've left the company. Avoid speaking negatively about your former employer or your colleagues, whether in private conversations or on social media. A good reputation is one of your most valuable assets, and taking care of it will benefit you throughout your career.

Quitting your job to pursue your entrepreneurial dreams is an exciting step, but it also requires care and planning. How you manage this transition will not only impact your present, but also the opportunities that come your way in the future. Exiting in a professional manner, with gratitude and respect, is the best way to start this new stage of your life on the right foot.

The First Year of Entrepreneurship

The first year of entrepreneurship is a mix of excitement, uncertainty, and constant learning. It's the time when your ideas meet reality, where you figure out what works and what needs to be adjusted. During this time, it's easy to feel overwhelmed, but it's also a time full of opportunities to grow and build the foundations of your business. To navigate this period successfully, you need to be prepared to face challenges, stay flexible, and stay focused on your goals.

One of the first challenges you'll face is managing your time. When you're self-employed, there's no boss telling you what to do or when to do it. This may feel liberating, but it also means you're completely responsible for how you use your hours. It's crucial to set a clear schedule and stick to it. Define your daily priorities, allocate time for the most important tasks, and avoid distractions. Learning to manage your time effectively can make the difference between making progress toward your goals or getting stuck in chaos.

Revenue flow will also be a challenge during the first year. Your earnings may not be consistent at first, and you will have to learn to manage financial uncertainty. For this reason, it is essential that you remain very disciplined with your spending. Keep a tight control of your budget and prioritize investments that are truly necessary for the growth of your business. This is not the time to spend impulsively, but to be strategic with every financial decision you make.

Loneliness can be another difficult aspect of this stage. If you're used to working in an environment full of colleagues, it can be a drastic change to find yourself alone most of the time. Look to build a support network, whether it's by connecting with other entrepreneurs, attending events related to your industry, or participating in online communities. Talking to people who share your experiences will not only help you feel less isolated, but it can also provide you with valuable ideas and new perspectives.

Another crucial aspect during the first year is adaptability. Not everything will go as planned, and there will be times when you will need to adjust your strategy. Listen to your customers, pay attention to the market, and don't be afraid to make changes if necessary. Rigidity can be a dangerous trap; flexibility, on the other hand, will allow you to respond quickly to challenges and take advantage of opportunities that arise.

Relationship building will be key to your early success. This includes not only your clients, but also suppliers, potential partners, and others within your industry. Treat every interaction as an opportunity to strengthen your professional network. Be genuine, trustworthy, and show real interest in the needs of the people you work with. A solid reputation can open doors for you and help establish you as a trusted figure in your industry.

Marketing your business will be one of your main tasks during this first year. It doesn't matter how great your product or service is if no one knows it exists. Define who your ideal customer is and use marketing strategies to reach them. This can include social media, advertising, public relations, or simply word of mouth. Experiment with different tactics and see which ones are most effective for your business. Remember that building a recognized brand takes time, but every little step counts.

It's also essential to take care of yourself during this time. Stress and long work hours can take a toll if you don't take care of yourself physically and mentally. Make sure you set aside time for rest, exercise, and healthy eating. Take time to unwind and enjoy activities that make you happy. Balance is important to maintain your energy and mental clarity, which will, in turn, be reflected in the quality of your work.

Constantly evaluate your progress. Set clear goals from the start and regularly review how close you are to achieving them. Not only will this help you stay focused, but it will also allow you to identify areas where you need to improve. If something isn't working, don't see it as a failure, but rather as an opportunity to learn and grow. The first year of entrepreneurship is, above all, a process of discovery.

Lastly, celebrate your accomplishments, no matter how small. Every client won, every project completed, and every obstacle overcome is a step toward your ultimate goal. Acknowledging your progress will not only keep you motivated, but it will also remind you why you decided to set out in the first place. This is a journey you chose because you believe in your vision and your ability to make it a reality.

The first year of entrepreneurship will be challenging, but it will also be one of the most significant in your journey. It is the time when you will lay the foundation for everything that will come next. Approach this stage with determination, curiosity, and patience. If you commit to learning, adapting, and persevering, you will be building not only a business, but also a stronger and more resilient version of yourself.

Scaling the Business Without Losing Your Mind

Scaling a business is one of the most exciting and challenging stages of your entrepreneurial journey. After you've laid the groundwork and achieved some stability, it's time to take your project to the next level. This involves increasing your operations, reaching more customers, and in many cases, taking on greater risks. However, growth isn't always easy. If you don't handle it carefully, it can become a source of stress and problems that threaten not only the health of your business, but also your personal well-being.

The first step to scaling a business without losing your mind is to get clear on why you want to grow. Not all growth is good or necessary. If you decide to expand simply because it seems to be what all successful businesses do, you might find yourself facing more problems than you expected. Evaluate whether growth is really aligned with your long-term goals. Ask yourself what kind of business you want to build and how that growth will contribute to your vision.

One of the biggest challenges when scaling a business is managing resources. As you grow, you'll need more time, money, and staff to keep up. This is where strategic planning becomes crucial. Before you take the next step, come up with a detailed plan that looks at how you'll manage these resources. Clearly define how much you can invest, how much additional load you can handle, and what processes you need to streamline to keep everything running smoothly.

Delegating will be your best ally. As your business grows, you won't be able to do everything yourself. Trying to take on every task and make every decision will not only exhaust you, but it will also limit your company's potential. Hire skilled people who share your values and trust them to carry out their responsibilities. Building a strong team is essential to scaling effectively. The key is finding the balance between delegating and maintaining reasonable control over operations.

Technology can be a powerful tool for growth. Automating repetitive processes, implementing efficient management systems, and using digital platforms to reach more customers are all effective ways to scale without adding too much stress to your day-to-day. However, it's not about adopting any technology available, but rather finding those that truly fit the needs of your business. Take the time to research, test, and evaluate which tools are the most suitable.

Communication also plays a key role. As your team grows, it's easy for connections to become lost and tasks to fall out of alignment with the overall vision. Establish clear channels of communication and make sure everyone is on the same page. Hold regular meetings, set concrete goals, and provide feedback consistently. Effective communication not only keeps your team focused, but it also reduces unnecessary misunderstandings and conflicts.

Another critical aspect of scaling is maintaining a good relationship with your customers. It's easy to become obsessed with attracting new buyers and neglect the ones who already trust you. However, your current customers are an invaluable source of revenue, referrals, and loyalty. Invest in strengthening that relationship, listen to their needs, and constantly work to improve their experience. A satisfied customer is the best advertising you can have.

Growth can also test your ability to handle stress. As you take on greater responsibilities and face more complex challenges, it's crucial that you don't neglect your mental and physical health. Set clear boundaries between your personal and professional life, and make time for activities that help you recharge. Whether it's exercise, spending time with loved ones, or simply resting, these practices are essential to keeping you balanced.

Finally, don't lose sight of your principles and values. Growth can bring with it the temptation to cut corners or compromise your standards to get quick results. Resist that temptation. Building a sustainable and ethical business for the long term is far more important than achieving an immediate goal. Stay true to what you believe in and make sure every decision you make reflects your company's values.

Scaling a business is an exciting process, but it's also an exercise in patience, strategy, and discipline. Don't try to do everything at once or compare yourself to others who seem to be going faster. Growth should be sustainable, both for your business and for yourself. By planning carefully, trusting the right people, and prioritizing the well-being of everyone involved, you can take your business to the next level without sacrificing your peace of mind or your purpose.

Smart Success

Smart success isn't about working tirelessly or sacrificing everything along the way. It's the ability to achieve your goals in an efficient, strategic, and balanced way, while enjoying the process and protecting what really matters in life. Many people associate success with long hours, constant stress, and an endless to-do list, but the truth is that there are more effective and sustainable ways to achieve it.

First, you need to understand that success is not one-size-fits-all. What success means to you may be very different from what it means to someone else. Maybe your idea of success is running a profitable business that allows you to spend more time with your family, or maybe it's building a global company that transforms an industry. The important thing is that you define what success means to you, clearly and honestly. Without this clarity, it's easy to lose your way by pursuing goals that don't fulfill you or that aren't aligned with your values.

One of the keys to smart success is prioritizing. You can't do it all, and you shouldn't try. Choose carefully where to focus your energy and resources. Identify which activities are truly driving your business forward and which are distractions that you could delegate, automate, or eliminate altogether. Not only will this mindset help you move faster, it will also reduce stress and allow you to spend time on what really matters.

Smart success also involves learning to say no. Along the way, many opportunities will arise that seem appealing, but not all of them will bring you closer to your goals. Every time you accept an unnecessary commitment, you are saying no to something more important. Carefully evaluate each decision and make sure it is aligned with your priorities. Saying no is not selfish, it is strategic.

Another key aspect is to continually learn. The world changes quickly, and what works today might not work tomorrow. Smart entrepreneurs spend time reading, studying, attending events, and surrounding themselves with people who inspire and challenge them to grow. This mindset of constant learning will not only keep you competitive, but it will also allow you to find creative solutions to the challenges you face.

Time management is another pillar of smart success. Your time is your most valuable resource, and how you use it will determine how far you go. Make it a habit to plan your days, set clear goals, and eliminate distractions. Don't confuse being busy with being productive. Often, doing less with greater quality and focus can be much more effective than trying to do everything at once.

Smart success is also about taking care of your health and well-being. An exhausted, stressed, or sick entrepreneur can't perform at their best. Make self-care a priority, not a luxury. This includes getting enough sleep, eating well, exercising, and taking regular breaks. Your energy and mental clarity are essential tools for success, so don't neglect them.

Surround yourself with people who share your vision and support you on your journey. Success doesn't happen alone. Building a strong team, establishing meaningful relationships, and learning from mentors are powerful strategies for moving forward. The right people will not only help you overcome obstacles, but they will also make the journey more rewarding and fulfilling.

Smart success also means knowing when to adapt. Not every idea works out the way you hoped, and not every strategy yields the desired results. Being flexible and willing to change course when necessary is an invaluable skill. Listen to the market, your customers, and your team, and adjust your plan accordingly. The ability to adapt to new circumstances can be the difference between stagnation and growth.

Finally, never lose sight of the purpose behind what you do. It's easy to get caught up in the day-to-day and forget why you started this journey in the first place. Remember that success isn't just measured in numbers or external achievements, but also in how you feel about your life and work. Find ways to enjoy the process, celebrate your accomplishments, and keep a balance between your professional and personal goals.

Smart success is the result of conscious decisions, discipline, and a strategic approach. It's not a race against time or a competition with others. It's a path you build your own way, by your own rules, as you create a life and business that reflects your values and aspirations. If you stay focused, flexible, and committed, you'll not only achieve your goals, but also enjoy the ride.

Henry Allen